TOP SPEEDS

HORSE — 75 KM (46 MILES) PER HOUR

ELECTRIC SKATEBOARD — 37 KM (23 MILES) PER HOUR

DOG — 70 KM (43.5 MILES) PER HOUR

RACING CAR — 360 KM (225 MILES) PER HOUR   NOW THAT'S FAST!: RACING CARS

RABBIT — 72 KM (45 MILES) PER HOUR

HUMAN — 45 KM (28 MILES) PER HOUR

BICYCLE — 132 KM (82 MILES) PER HOUR

NOW THAT'S FAST!
RACING CARS

KATE RIGGS

FRANKLIN WATTS
LONDON • SYDNEY

First published in the UK in 2011 by
Franklin Watts
338 Euston Road
London NW1 3BH

Franklin Watts Australia
Level 17/207 Kent Street
Sydney NSW 2000

First published by Creative Education,
an imprint of the Creative Company.
Copyright © 2010 Creative Education
International copyright reserved in all countries.
No part of this book may be reproduced in any
form without written permission from
the publisher.

All rights reserved.

ISBN 978 1 4451 0587 1
Dewey number: 629.2'28

A CIP catalogue record for this book
is available from the British Library.

Printed in China

Franklin Watts is a division of
Hachette Children's Books,
an Hachette UK company.
www.hachette.co.uk

Book and cover design by Blue Design
(www.bluedes.com)
Art direction by Rita Marshall

Photographs by Alamy (Pete Klinger/PCN
Photography), Corbis (Bettmann, Schlegelmilch),
Getty Images (DAVID BOILY/AFP, Michael Bradley,
Jonathan Ferrey, Robert Laberge, Mark Thompson,
Alvis Upitis), iStockphoto (Markus Seidel, Dieter
Spears), Shutterstock (Sergei Bachlakov, Chen
Wei Seng)

Every atttempt has been made to clear copyright.
Should there be any inadvertent omission, please
contact the publisher for rectification.

Racing cars are the fastest type of car. They have **bodies** and **engines** that have been specially **designed** to make them go as fast as possible. Many racing cars can zoom along at speeds of over 350 kilometres per hour (kph).

Racing cars are low to the ground. The air flows over them, pushing them down, so they can go faster.

People started racing cars in the 19th century. The first race took place in France in 1894 between the cities of Paris and Rouen. Twenty-five cars started the race, and the winning car crossed the finish line nearly seven hours later at an average speed of 19 kph!

An early car race in the USA.

RACING CARS

Most racing cars are **open-wheel** cars. Their wheels are much bigger than those on normal cars, and they are found on the outside of the car's body. Open-wheel cars are designed to be light and **aerodynamic**, which means that they go even faster!

10

Open-wheel cars can take tight turns while going at high speeds.

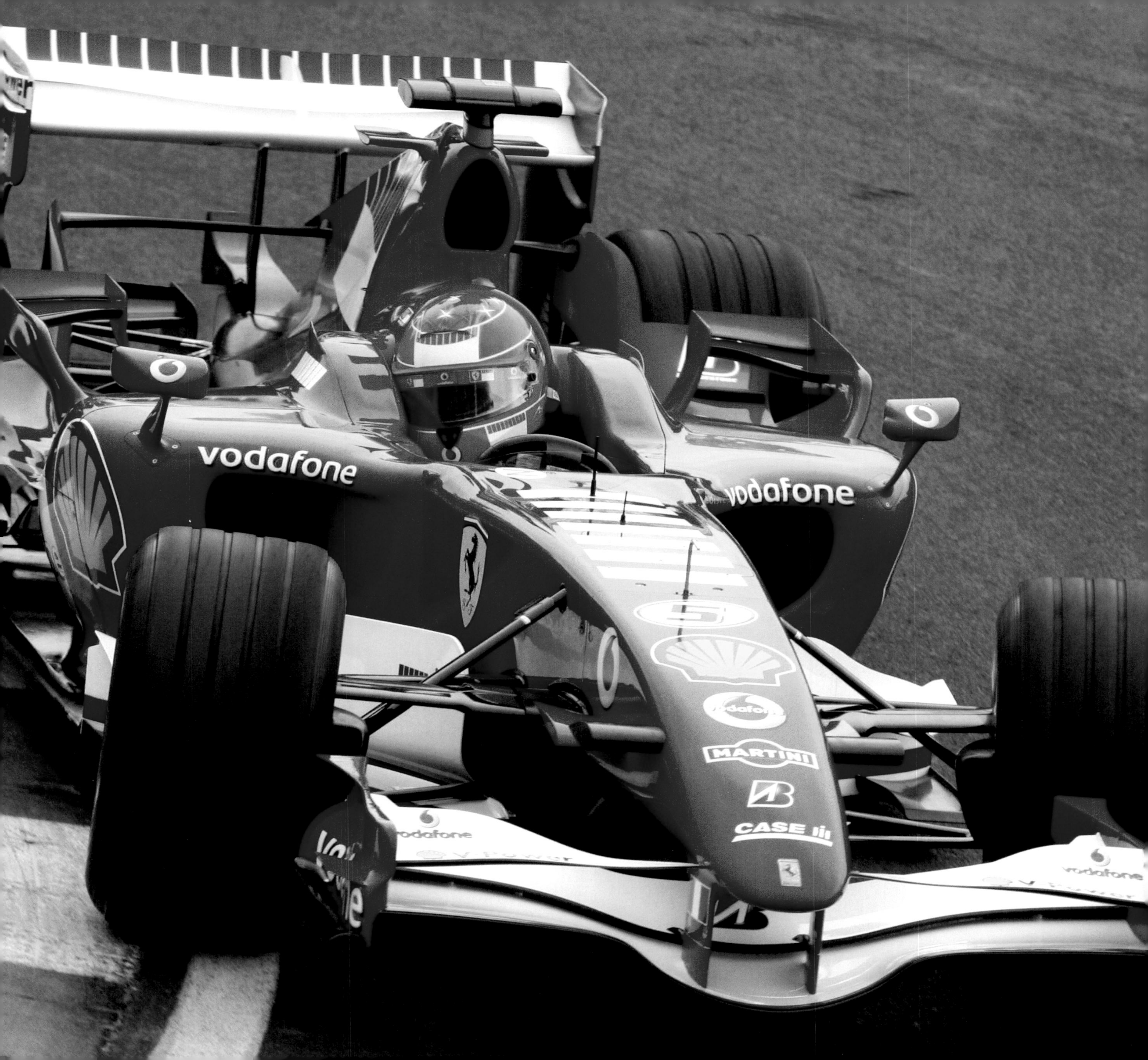
vodafone
vodafone
5
MARTINI
CASE

Around the world, Formula 1 is the best-known open-wheel car race series. Formula 1 cars compete in races called Grand Prix (*GRAN PREE*). There are about 20 races in each Formula 1 season. Drivers are awarded points according to where they finish in each race.

In the USA, Indy cars are the most popular open-wheel racing cars. They are named after the famous Indy 500 race in Indianapolis, where cars **compete** over 500 miles (800 kilometres) of tense, exciting action.

In both Formula 1 and Indy car racing, drivers make scheduled **pit stops**. During these breaks, the car tyres are changed and any quick repairs are made by the pit **crew**. The average pit stop lasts just a few seconds, then it's on with the race!

Formula 1 driver Lewis Hamilton makes a pit stop at the Malaysian Grand Prix.

RACING CARS

Other open-wheel race cars
are called sprints, midgets and
dragsters (above). Many sprint
cars do not have wings. Midgets
are very small race cars. Dragsters
look more like normal cars,
but have been specially
adapted for racing.

Midget cars are small, but powerful.
They are mainly raced over short
distances of 4 to 40 km.

In any kind of car racing, the driver's safety is very important. In open-wheel cars, the driver sits in a small **cockpit**. The cockpit does not cover the driver's head. Instead, drivers have to wear strong helmets to protect their heads.

Only one person at a time can drive an open-wheel racing car.

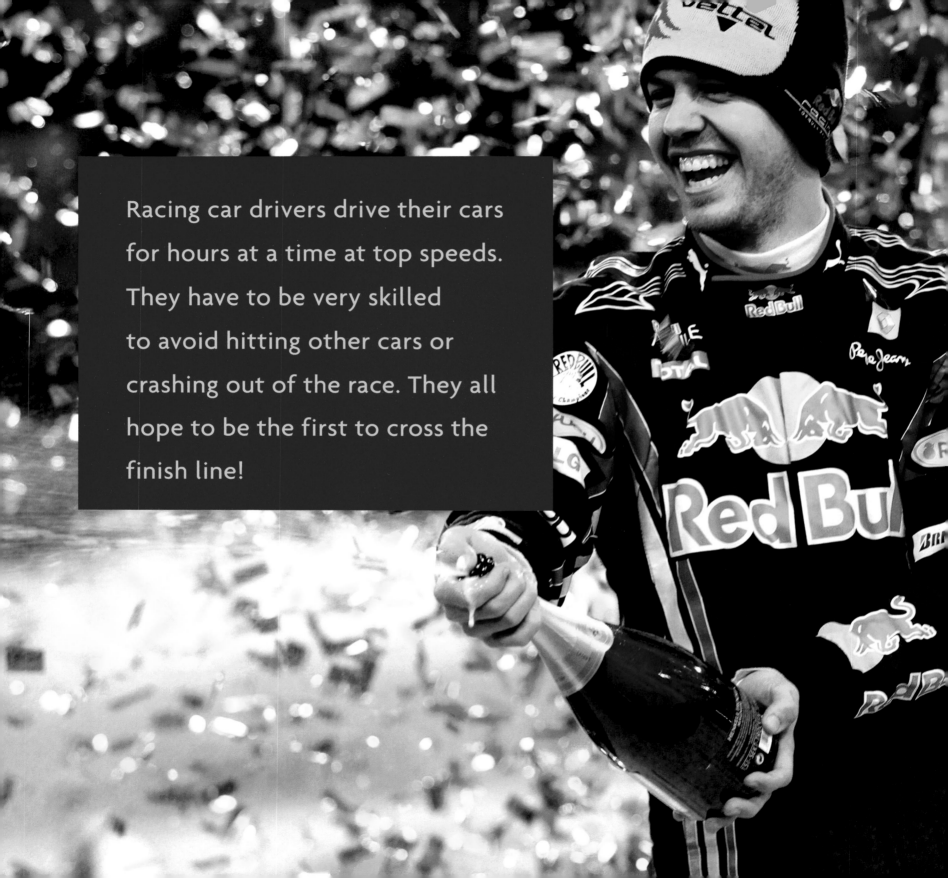

Racing car drivers drive their cars for hours at a time at top speeds. They have to be very skilled to avoid hitting other cars or crashing out of the race. They all hope to be the first to cross the finish line!

Fast Facts

An Indy car is allowed up to 28 new tyres for 320 km races, and 60 new tyres for 800 km races. That's a lot of pit stops!

Indy cars run on methanol, a wood-based alcohol. Methanol is a safer fuel because it is not **flammable**.

A Formula 1 car is made up of around 80,000 different parts.

The average Formula 1 car can accelerate from 0 to 160 kph and back to 0 in just four seconds!

On average, a Formula 1 driver loses about four kilograms in weight during each race.

Glossary

aerodynamic – able to cut through the air easily

body – the main part of something

cockpit – the place where the driver sits in a race car or aeroplane

compete – to try to win something

crew – a team of workers, such as mechanics

design – to plan how something will look and how it will work

engines – machines inside vehicles that make them move

flammable – able to catch fire

open-wheel – where the wheels are on the outside of the car's body

pit stop – when a racing car comes off the track so that the crew can make repairs to, change a tyre or re-fuel the car

Read More about It

Motormania: Racing Cars
Penny Worms (Franklin Watts, 2010)
Mega Machine Drivers: This Is My Racing Car
Chris Oxlade (Franklin Watts, 2009)

Website

QuarterMidgets.com's racing activities for kids
http://www.quartermidgets.com/kids_activities/index.htm
This site has activities such as colouring pages.

Index

cockpits 21
drivers 13, 21, 22
engines 6
first race 8
Formula 1 . . . . .12, 13, 17, 23
Grand Prix 13, 17
Indy 500 15
Indy cars 15, 17, 23
open-wheel cars 13, 15, 17, 18, 21
pit stops 17
safety 21
speeds 6, 8, 23